# Affirmation Alchemy

By

Dean Whiteside

Copyright © 2024 Dean Whiteside

ISBN: 978-1-916981-78-2

All rights reserved, including the right to reproduce this book, or portions thereof in any form. No part of this text may be reproduced, transmitted, downloaded, decompiled, reverse engineered, or stored, in any form or introduced into any information storage and retrieval system, in any form or by any means, whether electronic or mechanical without the express written permission of the author.

# Introduction

Hello and welcome. I am thrilled to be your guide on the journey through the pages of this transformative book. Over the past decade, I have worked in the fascinating world of vibration analysis, a field that deals with resonating vibration frequencies that are beyond the limits of human perception. Through this unique perspective, I've come to understand the profound truth in believing in the unseen. It was within this work I discovered that the law of attraction was indeed real.

In parallel with my work as a vibration analyst, I am also a dedicated practitioner of positive psychology. I've dedicated my time to helping individuals cultivate a positive-biased lifestyle, with the aim of unlocking their full potential. A lifestyle where living on the same frequency as optimism and positivity become the driving forces behind personal growth and fulfilment.

As I dived deeper into these seemingly disparate worlds of vibrational analysis and positive psychology, an incredibly profound connection became clear to me. The law of attraction, a principle associated with manifesting one's desires into reality, was intricately linked to the vibrational energies that I had been studying and working with for years within both fields.

This realisation led me to a fascinating journey of research and exploration. I set out to uncover the perfect, and in my opinion, the *only* way to construct an affirmation that triggers the law of attraction in your favour. This powerful framework of words is constructed in a way that can effortlessly harness the attraction process, and will put you on—and more importantly keep you on—the same resonating frequency as your desires, so that they can magnetically pull into your reality.

Through the fusion of my experience as a vibration analyst and positive psychology practitioner, and after years of extensive personal research, I've uncovered the secret and science behind creating an affirmation that can transform your life.

In the pages that follow, I will share with you the culmination of this profound journey, providing you with the toolbox and insight you require to access the unseen natural resonating energies of the universe and unlock the effortless power of manifestation. This is the world where the unseen becomes your greatest ally, and the law of attraction becomes your most trusted companion.

Before we start our journey, in this book we first cover the science and reasoning behind the affirmation technique that will empower you to access the law of attraction in your favour. To harness the full effectiveness of this process, it's crucial not to skip any content prior to getting to the affirmation itself. Try not to be tempted to jump to the end. It's essential you read it all the way through. Doing this will cement your confidence in the whole process, making it easier to implement into your life.

We will explore the research and discoveries that underpin this powerful roadmap to *Affirmation Alchemy*. I'll provide you with the knowledge and understanding of why this technique works, enabling you to embrace it with total confidence and conviction.

Now, while the content may seem extensive at times, remember that it is designed to illuminate the origins of this transformational approach. I want you to appreciate the science and logic behind the method, ensuring you have a solid foundation before diving into practice.

I assure you, at the end of this book you'll discover an effortless and straightforward practical technique that you can begin using immediately to kickstart your journey and keep you on the same frequency of what you desire. This technique has been carefully crafted to simplify the process and access the law of attraction in your favour, allowing you to implement it seamlessly into your daily life.

**\*Note:**

The key is to try and not feel overwhelmed as you explore the information within these pages. Consider it your blueprint to understanding the "why" behind the technique.

Let's begin your journey to becoming an *Affirmation Alchemist*.

# Vibration Continued

In my role as a vibration analysis engineer, I spent over a decade immersed in the unseen energies that dictate the harmony or havoc within machinery.

Little did I anticipate that within the world of rotating components and vibrating structures, I would unearth a profound realisation about the realism of our existence—energies attract each other when they resonate on the same frequency.

Every day I engaged in the meticulous job of ensuring that machines and structures did not share resonant frequencies, a task like preventing two magnets from snapping together with irresistible force.

It was in this intricacy of this role as a vibration analyst that the law of attraction unfolded before my eyes, not in the personal realm, but in the realm of physics, the realm of reality.

If a machine and a structure I was working on shared the same resonant frequency, their energies would synchronously attract, creating a magnetic force so powerful that it could lead to the physical destruction of both. I vividly recall an incident where a machine, having fallen into resonance with its host structure, exerted a magnetic force so strong that it shattered the holding bolts designed to withstand eight tonnes of pressure. The longer they resonated together, the more intense the shared energy became. It was in that moment the law of attraction became very real to me.

In this technical ballet, the parallels with the law of attraction became glaringly evident. It dawned on me that shared energy, attraction, and resonance were not mystical concepts, but principles grounded in physics. I observed that, much like machinery, the longer thoughts and emotions (because thoughts and emotions emit a vibration frequency) resonated with the frequencies of our desires (because everything that exists has a natural resonating frequency) the more powerful the force of attraction. It was physics, not fiction.

That realisation sparked a mission within me—to bridge the gap between the mechanics of the machinery I was working with, and the manifestation of desires. It marked the genesis of my obsession with exploring how affirmations, like alchemical spells, could trigger thoughts and emotions that not only resonated, but more importantly stayed on the same frequency as our aspirations. I wanted to decipher the alchemy of crafting words into reality, leading to the creation of a pathway that seamlessly aligned the frequencies of our feelings and emotions with the things we want in life—affirmation alchemy.

# Positive Psychology + Vibration

Continuing the topic from the previous chapter. Vibration resonance in machines is a straightforward application of physics. Matching the running frequency of a machine to the resonating frequency of the structure it's attached to ensures a seamless sharing of attracting energy. This process can be initiated, maintained, and halted with remarkable ease. If the frequencies need adjustment, a simple manual alteration achieves the desired result.

However, when we dive into the intricate landscape of human thought and emotion, it's apparent that our conscious nature complicates the resonance process.

Unlike machines, we are not as adept at sustaining a constant frequency, primarily due to the intricate nature of our consciousness. This complexity arises from our inherent tendency to give heightened attention to negative events and experiences—a phenomenon underscored by Positive Psychology, a field that focuses on what goes right, rather than what goes wrong. This negativity bias, where we allocate five times more focus to negative occurrences than positive ones, sheds light on the challenges individuals face when embarking on the journey of self-creation.

For those of us who are constantly grappling with the day-to-day challenge of tipping the scales towards positivity, the formidable reality of our natural negativity bias, which holds a potency five times greater, can inadvertently lock us into the repetitive frequency of a life towards negativity. This habitual resonance with a negative matching energy serves as a huge obstacle, explaining why some individuals find themselves distanced from the life they aspire to lead.

The continuous flow of negative energy, sculpted by our minds, becomes a magnetic force—identical to the attracting force between a machine and its structure—pulling opportunities of consistent negativity into our lives.

Understanding this intricate interplay starts to explain the reasons behind the difference between our desired life and our current reality.

The crux of self-creation and success lies in maintaining the same vibrational state as the desired outcome, resonating on the same frequency long enough to witness the manifestation of the things that we do want to attract unfold—it is a task easier said than done. The pitfall arises when external factors alter our frequency naturally, introducing elements like limiting beliefs, attachment to specific outcomes, and the powerful emotion of needing something in order to be happy. The latter, in particular, is a formidable negative frequency that can undermine the very essence of positive attraction. These all correspond with our natural negativity bias, and it is these obstacles that are a hindrance to you creating the life you want.

The specifically crafted affirmation in this book is a tool designed to navigate the intricacies of resonance for the things you want in life, based on a physics approach.

It's constructed with precision to trigger instinctive elaboration reflex (I will explain more on this in the following pages).

And this affirmation redirects focus on solutions and effortlessly detaches from the emotionally charged state of needing. It's a nuanced approach aimed at harmonising thought and emotion frequencies, aligning them with the desired outcome while mitigating the influences that can lead to deviation.

#  Manifesting Miracles

In this section, I will share a glimpse of the remarkable manifestations that have occurred in my life, thanks to a decade-long dedication in finding the hack to personally creating my own dreams.

The following examples are just a fraction of what I continue to achieve on my personal journey. I have too many to list in one book!

*My Dream Home*:

As a child, I always dreamed of living on a specific street. Despite two rejections while trying to buy a particular house there, I persisted, knowing I resonated with the desire to live on that street. By maintaining that frequency, I attracted the opportunity, and a few months later, I was offered the exact same house I had previously been rejected from on that very street.

*Creating Opportunities*:

A decade ago, diving into this world of self-creation, I crafted a unique role within the company I worked for, previously non-existent. Desiring a specific position focusing on vibration analysis due to its connection to the law of attraction, I materialised this idea into an opportunity. Sustaining the same vibrational frequency, a few months later, a new job role aligned with my desire was announced in a weekly meeting. I seized the opportunity that presented itself, and applied for and secured the position, which not only fulfilled my aspirations but also brought a substantial pay rise and reduced working hours. This experience underscored the transformative power of accurate affirmations that keep you on the same resonant frequency as your desire, manifesting seemingly impossible opportunities.

*Investment for Well-Being*:

I secured investment for a community well-being project by applying the attraction principles I had studied for years while running local positivity classes. One day, a text message revealed an opportunity at my local doctor's surgery seeking volunteers for well-being assistance, with a chance to apply for funding. Grasping this opportunity as it presented itself, I got accepted for the funding, showcasing the power to attract resources for positive change.

*Radio Show Appearance*:

A childhood dream materialised when I became a guest on a radio show, a goal nurtured since my fondness for radio in my youth. I set the objective to appear on a show, applied my process, maintained the frequency, and one day, during training at my former amateur boxing club, the head coach presented an opportunity to promote the club on a BBC radio sports show, inviting me to be one of the featured boxers. This showcases yet another manifestation achieved through the self-creation process.

*Dream Trip to Rome*:

Having always wanted to visit Italy, particularly Rome for my love of coffee and Italian culture, I set a goal to sit outside a traditional coffee shop there. Applying my process, resonating on the same frequency, a short while later, my line manager approached me during my work in the new role I created as a vibration analyst. They offered an all-expenses-paid work trip to another company factory, without specifying the location. Accepting the opportunity, I later learned it was the factory in Italy, spending one night in Pescara and two days in Rome. Only two hours were spent in the factory during the three-day trip, and the rest was free time. This attracted desire not only came true but was fully funded, emerging as my favourite travel experience among many others attracted into my life.

*Finding My Dream Partner*:

Against all odds, I attracted my dream partner in an almost impossible circumstance. Deciding to attract my ideal companion, I initiated my process, leveraging real-life knowledge of vibration frequencies from my job. Remarkably, I knew the exact type of person I desired, based on a connection I had with someone seven years prior. Having met a girl at the gym, we shared a few memorable months together. Although she worked overseas and we parted ways when she returned, I couldn't ignore the connection. Seven years later, I set my goal to meet someone exactly like her. About six months after setting this goal, I unexpectedly encountered my dream partner—the very same person I had met years ago in the same gym. We reconnected, and we've been together ever since. This serves as proof that there are no limits or barriers to achieving our dreams, only those we choose to impose on ourselves.

*A Thriving Business*:

Attracting my own business marked a pinnacle in my journey of using the law of attraction to shape my reality. While working for a company, I aspired to lead a life with a flexible schedule, managing my own business and choosing my workdays. Having set this goal, I employed my knowledge of vibration frequencies again to align myself with this desire. Unexpectedly, an old friend offered to help me set up a business, requiring me to leave a secure salaried job and take the leap into entrepreneurship. Seizing the opportunity presented by the law of attraction process, not only did my own business instantly boost my monthly income by more than two and a half times compared to any previous salaried job, but it also granted me the gift of freedom and time. I only worked the days I wanted to. This showcased the transformative power of manifestation in the professional sector.

These handpicked examples only serve as a mere glimpse into the incredible manifestations that I have achieved throughout my own personal journey over the years of self-creation. I chose these because they show a diversity of things that you can create for your own reality. My list continues to grow.

These illustrate the potential of the affirmation technique discussed in this book to shape destinies, overcome obstacles, and bring forth our deepest desires.

As we continue this journey together, remember that these are just a small example, and your own affirmations journey can unlock a world of possibilities beyond your imagination.

# Rediscovering Your Confidence in Creation

Now, if you've purchased this book, it's probably because you already possess an interest in the concept of the law of attraction. Perhaps you've even experienced moments in your life when you've seen this phenomenon at work, times where your thoughts and intentions seemed to shape your reality.

However, somewhere along the way, you might have lost a bit of confidence in the process.

This chapter is designed to reignite that confidence and empower you to attract your desires with renewed belief and understanding. Let's embark on an exercise that will serve as a reminder of your past successes in manifesting reality.

**Exercise:** *Your Proof of Manifestation*

Take a moment to reflect and make a list of all the things that, at one point in your life, you considered impossible but have since achieved.

These could be minor or major achievements, personal or professional, or anything in between.

As you compile your list, consider moments when you wished for something, forgot about it, and eventually saw it come to fruition.

Reflect on the times when your thoughts and intentions aligned with the events in your life.

Once you have your list formulated, take some time to read through it carefully. Each item on that list is a testament to your ability to create your own reality. It is proof that you've been a conscious creator, shaping your life in ways you may not have fully acknowledged. Remember that these were the moments that you stayed on the frequency of your desire long enough for it to come to fruition.

This exercise is not only about celebrating your past successes but also about reaffirming your innate ability to manifest your desires. It's a reminder that you've experienced the law of attraction in action, maybe without even noticing, and with the right knowledge and technique, you can continue to do so in a deliberate and intentional manner.

As you progress through this book, let this exercise serve as a foundation for your renewed confidence in the power of manifestation. You've already witnessed the magic; now, it's time to unlock its full potential in your life.

# Wanting vs Needing

## Wanting vs Needing: *The Power of Desire and Detachment*

In this section, we will explore a fundamental concept in the attraction process—the difference between wanting and needing. It's essential to understand that wanting is a natural and healthy part of human existence. Wanting gives us drive to set goals, dream big, and strive for personal growth. However, when we transition from wanting to believing we need something to be happy, it can create a scarcity mindset that hinders our ability to attract the things we want.

We will also dive into the importance of detachment from outcomes and how the specific affirmation technique presented in this book simplifies this process.

*The Power of Wanting*:

Desire is a powerful force. It fuels our ambitions, motivates us to act, and adds excitement to our lives. There is absolutely nothing wrong with wanting something. In fact, wanting is the catalyst for change and growth. When we want something, we set our sights on it and work diligently to achieve it. This is where motivation and the energy to pursue our goals comes from.

*The Pitfall of Believing We Need*:

The shift from wanting to believing we need something in order to be happy can be a slippery slope. When we convince ourselves that we can't be content without a specific outcome, we inadvertently create a sense of lack and scarcity in our lives. This scarcity mindset can cause our subconscious to focus on what we lack, ultimately attracting more of the same, because we are resonating on the scarcity frequency.

It's vital to recognise that your happiness and fulfilment should not be dependent on external circumstances. This is why, when crafting scripts and affirmations that you speak to yourself regarding the things that you want in life, there should be an element of detachment from the outcome within them.

*The Importance of Detachment*:

Detachment is the key to successful manifestation. It means allowing yourself to want something while simultaneously letting go of the need for it. When you are detached from the outcome, you free yourself from anxiety and desperation, which can repel your desires. Detachment allows you to maintain a sense of peace and trust in the process, knowing that what is meant for you will come to you. Getting good at detachment in this way is what keeps you on the desired frequency of your goal.

*The Affirmation Technique and Detachment*:

The law of attraction technique presented in this book is designed to take the guesswork out of the attraction process. It is structured to incorporate detachment seamlessly into your affirmations. By affirming your desires with detachment, you release resistance and allow the universe to work its laws of vibration and energy in your favour.

The affirmation process this book provides helps you strike the balance between wanting and needing, ensuring you stay motivated while remaining at peace with whatever unfolds.

Understanding the difference between wanting and needing is crucial in your journey towards attracting your goals. While wanting is healthy and motivating, needing can create a scarcity mindset that hinders your progress. Detachment from outcomes is equally essential, as it allows you to trust the process and maintain peace regardless of the results. The affirmation technique shared in this book is your tool for effortlessly incorporating detachment into your manifesting practice. Embrace the power of wanting, let go of the need, and watch your desires attract with ease.

# Detachment Exercise

Exercise: *The "Want vs Need" Jar*

To reinforce the distinction between wanting and needing, let's engage in a practical exercise that will help you develop this essential mindset. Grab a pen and some paper, and follow these steps:

1. *Label Your Paper*:

At the top of your paper, write "Wants."

2. *Prepare a Jar*:

Find a jar or container of your choice, and label it "Not Needs."

3. *List Your Desires*:

Start listing down as many things as you want in life. These can be material possessions, experiences, achievements, or any desires you have in mind. The key here is to focus on things you genuinely want in life.

4. *Transfer to the "Not Needs" Jar*:

After you've completed your list of wants, cut or tear the paper into individual slips, each containing one desire. Then, place these slips into the "Not Needs" jar.

5. *Let Go and Forget*:

Once all your desires are in the jar, close the lid and put it away somewhere safe. This exercise is not meant to be an ongoing practice like the manifestation technique in this book. It's a one-time exercise designed to help you distinguish the feeling between wanting and needing. So, forget about the contents of the jar for now.

6. *Reflect on the Difference*:

Over time, as you go about your daily life, reflect on the fact that your wants are in the "Not Needs" jar. This serves as a reminder that you can desire things without attaching a sense of necessity to them.

Remember, this exercise is a training tool to help you internalise the concept of wanting without needing. It's designed to help you practise not relying on external things to make you happy. I know this may appear counterintuitive, but trust me, the more you let go of needing something in your life, the faster it navigates to you.

The affirmation process presented in this book simplifies the process and incorporates this understanding seamlessly. By practicing this exercise, you'll build the foundation for a healthier relationship with your desires and a deeper appreciation of the power of detachment.

# Why "I Am" Doesn't Work

In this chapter, we'll explore the world of "I am" affirmations and why they may not be working for you.

You've likely heard that "I am" affirmations can be transformational, but if you've found them ineffective, you're not alone. So, let's explore why, and how we can construct an affirmation that will trigger belief and pave the way for powerful manifestation.

*The Limitations of Statements*:

Statements are often considered assertive, telling sentences. When you repeat "I am" followed by a statement like "I am confident," it's like stating a fact. However, if deep down you don't believe that statement to be true (which is why you're using the affirmation in the first place), it can create a contradiction in your subconscious.

*The Subconscious Belief*:

Your subconscious mind holds your core beliefs, and if it contradicts an affirmation, your core belief remains unaltered. For instance, if you repeatedly say, "I am confident" but your subconscious holds the core belief "I don't believe I'm confident," the latter is what tends to prevail.

*The Importance of Belief and Imagination*:

To create lasting change through affirmations, we must bridge the gap between what we consciously say and what we subconsciously believe. The missing link here is imagination. If you can't vividly imagine or visualise the reality of your affirmation, it's challenging to bypass the resistance of your subconscious.

*My Revelation*:

In my personal journey, I had a significant revelation. I realised that affirmations had to be constructed in a way that instantly triggers belief without room for doubt. The key lies in crafting an affirmation that will engage your imagination and align with your core beliefs, effectively rewiring your subconscious to enable you to effectively visualise your desired outcome.

*The Evolution of Affirmations*:

Affirmations should be more than mere statements. They should be open-ended, inviting your imagination to participate actively.

*Instant Belief, Lasting Change*:

By scripting an affirmation that can trigger instant belief and involve your imagination, you create a bridge between your conscious desires and subconscious beliefs. This alignment paves the way for powerful attraction, as there is no contradiction to overcome. It's a harmonious journey towards your goals.

So, in conclusion, affirmations can indeed be transformational, but only when they are constructed in a way that engages your imagination, aligns with your core beliefs, and keeps you on the same resonating frequency as your goal. By evolving your affirmations beyond flat statements, you open the door to belief, paving the way for lasting change and powerful attraction. In the following pages, we'll dive deeper into the technique of creating such affirmations and integrating them seamlessly into your life.

# Affirmation Exercise

**Exercise:** *The Mirror Affirmation Challenge*

Before we proceed, let's engage in an exercise that highlights the limitations of flat "I am" statements.

Find a mirror, look at your reflection, and follow these steps:

1. *Stand in Front of the Mirror*:

Find a quiet space where you can be alone with your reflection. Stand comfortably in front of the mirror.

2. *Gaze into Your Eyes*:

Look into your own eyes and make a connection with your own reflection.

3. *Say the Statement*:

In a clear voice, say the statement, "I am confident."

4. *Observe Your Reaction*:

Pay close attention to how you feel as you say this statement. Notice if it feels flat, emotionless, or lacks resonance with your inner self. Is there an emotional response, or does it feel disconnected?

5. *Reflect on Your Experience*:

After saying the statement, take a moment to reflect on your experience. What emotions, if any, did it trigger? Did it engage your imagination, or did it feel like a mere statement?

6. *Prepare for the Next Chapter*:

Once you've completed this exercise, you're ready to move on to the next chapter. We'll explore how to transform these flat "I am" statements into dynamic affirmations that engage your imagination and trigger genuine belief.

This exercise serves as a starting point for understanding the limitations of traditional "I am" affirmations.

# Making Affirmations Powerful

Transforming Affirmations: *The Power of Question-Based Affirmations*

In our quest to make affirmations more effective and aligned with our desires, we've reached a pivotal turning point. We're about to explore a transformational approach that shifts affirmations from flat statements to engaging questions. These question-based affirmations tap into the remarkable phenomenon known as "instinctive elaboration'' I mentioned earlier and provide us with a potent tool for manifestation.

*Understanding the Power of Questions*:

Questions are not just a form of communication; they are mental triggers that prompt a phenomenon known as "instinctive elaboration." When you ask yourself a question, your brain instinctively shifts into problem-solving mode, devoting its full attention to finding an answer. This mental reflex is a powerful tool for focusing your thoughts and engaging your imagination for visualisation.

*The Brain's Single-Focus Capacity*:

Neuroscientist John Medina's research highlights a critical fact: the human brain cannot truly multitask. Instead, it processes attention-rich inputs sequentially.

When a question is posed, it takes over your brain's thought process, and when your brain is thinking of the answer to a question, it cannot contemplate anything else. This leaves no room for simultaneous distractions. This singular focus is the key to harnessing the power of questions for affirmation alchemy.

*From Flat Statements to Dynamic Questions*:

Imagine transforming an affirmation like "I am confident" into a powerful question-based affirmation that takes over the brain's process, and therefore sending out the same vibration frequency of the thing you desire to attract into your life. How much more powerful do you think that could be?

In the future, instead of a flat statement, we could reframe them as powerful questions. This simple shift engages your imagination and triggers the brain's instinctive elaboration process, therefore putting its full focus on finding the solution.

*Bypassing the Subconscious*:

The magic of question-based affirmations lies in their ability to bypass the resistance of your subconscious mind. When you pose a question instead of an "I am" statement, your subconscious doesn't have the chance to doubt or reject it because your brain is too busy searching for an answer. This allows your affirmation to slip seamlessly into your subconscious, aligning your beliefs with your desires.

*The Coming Pages*:

In the upcoming pages, we will explore the art of crafting dynamic question-based affirmations that engage your imagination, trigger instant belief, and resonate on the same frequency as your goals.

You'll discover how to harness the full potential of this technique to access the law of attraction effortlessly.

As we dig deeper into the world of question-based affirmations, remember that the power to reshape your reality and create your own life lies within your questions, not your statements.

# How the Brain Finds Answers

The Brain's Problem-Solving Modes

Before we go into the art of crafting powerful question-based affirmations that trigger the law of attraction in your favour, it's essential to explore further the intriguing relationship between the brain and questions, and give you another reason why questions are the secret to powerful affirmations.

The way our brain solves problems has a direct impact on our ability to manifest and attract our desires.

*Two Ways of Finding Answers*:

As revealed in a captivating study discussed in the article Your Brain Has 2 Ways of Finding Answers. Which Is Best? | Inc.com our brains have two distinct modes for finding answers: analysis and insight. The study's results indicated that finding answers through insight were significantly more effective than through analysis.

*The Implication for Manifestation*:

So, what does this mean for our journey towards becoming "affirmation alchemists" and mastering the art of attracting our goals? It underscores the importance of not overanalysing the how and where of your manifestations. When you focus too intensely on dissecting the path your desire will take, you may inadvertently hinder the process. Focusing too much on the outcome will in fact take you off the frequency of your goal and therefore stop the resonating and sharing the matching energy.

*Letting Go of How it Will Happen*:

So, in the context of manifestation, it's crucial to understand that the process can often unfold in ways that are beyond our current understanding. Trying to map out every detail and forcing a specific outcome can limit the universe's ability to orchestrate events in your favour. This is where the importance of detachment comes into play. Detachment allows for insight to occur, and as the article shows, finding answers through insight was far more effective than through analysis.

Detaching from the outcome means letting go of rigid expectations and surrendering to the flow of the laws of vibration. It's about trusting that the process of energy attraction, guided by your question-based affirmations, will bring your desires to fruition in the most efficient way possible.

*Construction of Powerful Affirmations*:

In the following pages, we will explore how to construct question-based affirmations that not only engage your imagination and subconscious, but also align with the insights that your brain is naturally adept at generating. These affirmations will make it easier to lead you down the path of resonating on the same frequency of your desire with confidence, without the need to micromanage the details.

As you move forward, remember that the power of attracting what you want, and resonating on the same frequency as those things, is not just in asking questions, but in allowing the answers to flow naturally. Embrace the process, trust the journey, and watch your desires begin to come to fruition.

# The Magic Technique

The Magical Affirmation Technique: *Manifesting with Precision.*

So, we've arrived at the moment we've been building up to—the unveiling of the technique that will empower you to construct what I consider the *only* affirmations you need to attract magical outcomes. In this chapter, I'll walk you through the technique I've developed, breaking it down into its essential components.

*The Power of "What" and "How" Questions*:

The first transformational step in crafting your magical affirmation involves changing from an "I am" statement to a "What" or "How" question. The use of "What" and "How" in framing your question-based affirmation is intentional, as it encourages a solution-focused mindset. As we discussed in the previous chapter, the brain navigates the terrain of problem-solving through two distinct avenues: insight and analysis. The potency of using the words "What" and "How" in our affirmations lies in their open-ended nature within the context of a question.

This openness allows the brain to engage its innate ability for insight, tapping into a wellspring of creative solutions. If you're wondering why we don't use the word "Why" to start a question, the reason for that is, while possessing its own depth of power, it is fundamentally analytical. Therefore, in the art of crafting powerful affirmations, the emphasis on "What" and "How" serves as a deliberate choice to steer the mind towards insight, unlocking its creative potential for maximum effectiveness.

*Embracing Detachment from Outcome*:

As also previously discussed in the earlier pages, the element of wanting without needing is a vital aspect of effective manifestation. The next part of your affirmation is where you insert this essential component. It's the point where you detach from the outcome in advance, while releasing the need for it to materialise in a specific way. The balance between these creates the perfect environment for attraction to occur.

*Enter Your Desires*:

Having recited the affirmation to ignite your solution-focused mindset through instinctive elaboration and affirmed your detachment from outcomes, the subsequent vital step is to input your goals and desires. Your mind, finely tuned by the preceding steps, is now in an optimal state to immerse itself fully in the attraction process. I strongly advocate for the tangible act of putting pen to paper during this affirmation exercise, as it adds a powerful layer of effectiveness. However, in the absence of pen and paper, vividly run your wishes and desires through your mind, envisioning them with the intensity as if they were already your reality. This seamless transition into visualisation of your goals is facilitated by the groundwork laid in parts one and two, ensuring a fluid and effective manifestation process.

*The Magic Affirmation*:

This last step is the magic in this process. It involves the utterance of a distinct affirmation; this is the very affirmation we have been leading up to. It is crafted to anchor you firmly on the resonant frequency of your goal and keep you there. It's designed to not only maintain your alignment with the desired frequency but also to discourage any deviation from this crucial vibrational state, ensuring that your thoughts and emotions remain harmoniously attuned to the attraction of your goals, thereby solidifying the foundation for successful intentional creation.

What we've undertaken so far in this book has been the science behind crafting question-based affirmations that encompass detachment and encourage insight. It's a super simple technique that combines the power of desire, solution-focused thinking, and trust in the universe's ability to deliver your desires.

***Important Note:** *The below is a section of the book I want you to really focus on!*

In the vast landscape of the law of attraction and manifestation, it's crucial to dispel a common misconception that often leads to disappointment and scepticism. Let me be unequivocal—I don't subscribe to the notion that resonating on the same frequency as your goals delivers your desires conveniently to your doorstep without any effort on your part. Many books propagate this idea, and it's precisely this misinterpretation that breeds disillusionment and disbelief in the efficacy of the law of attraction.

Having witnessed the power of vibration frequencies, and resonating energy, within my job I assure you that the law of attraction is indeed real, albeit in a manner that demands our understanding and active participation.

So, how does the affirmation technique presented in this book unfold the magic of manifestation if not in the form of doorstep deliveries? The answer lies in a profound yet often overlooked concept: *it appears as opportunity!*

Whether your desire is for a thriving business or a transformative emotional outcome like increased confidence, the universe responds by conspiring with its energetic forces (no different to how it does within machinery). It resonates with the frequency of your desire and presents you with opportunities aligned with that resonance. However, it's crucial to comprehend that the universe doesn't hand you the desire itself; it is critically important to understand that it instead crafts a pathway, an opportunity for you to manifest the things that you want in life. It is then up to us to take advantage of this, and act on the opportunity that has been attracted.

Consider the example of wanting your own business. Using the affirmation technique will not magically replace your workday with the ownership of a business. Instead, the universe, in its grand orchestration, will resonate with your desire then attract and pull an opportunity for you to create your business.

The same principle applies to emotional manifestations—resonate with the frequency of confidence, and the universe will offer opportunities for you to express and build confidence, not the confidence itself.

Once you grasp this concept, your life will change, because, instead of wondering when and how the desire will arrive, you will go into every day actively looking for opportunities. This will aid in keeping you on the same resonant frequency of what you are trying to attract.

As I emphasised in the introduction chapters, the magnetic force of resonant frequencies is a powerful mechanism of attraction. The universe creates a pathway for your desires to materialise by presenting opportunities on the same frequency as your aspirations. However, the pivotal point: it is then your responsibility to act on these opportunities.

Take a moment to reflect on the most successful individuals; their remarkable achievements are not mere coincidence, but a result of their relentless commitment to action.

When the universe presents an opportunity aligned with their desires, they seize it without hesitation.

While I will cover the importance of action a little more in later pages, it's paramount for now to grasp that opportunities are the universe's way of upholding its end of the deal, and your role is to reciprocate by acting.

By approaching the law of attraction in this nuanced and accurate perspective, you will notice that it will become a journey filled with signs and synchronicities, not disappointment and wondering. You will feel the joy and excitement of witnessing your desires materialise through opportunities. Embrace this understanding, and you'll find your creation journey to be not only enjoyable but also incredibly transformative.

**Try it now:** *Signs and Synchronicities.*

Consider a moment in your life when a fleeting thought crossed your mind—perhaps about a specific thing. You let the thought dissipate, only to find, seemingly out of nowhere, instances related to that very thought begin to unfold in your reality.

Alternatively, have you ever ruminated on a friend or acquaintance, only to have them call or text you unexpectedly? These instances are not mere coincidences; they are the synchronicities orchestrated by the resonant frequency you remained on, delivering opportunities on that same vibrational state directly to you. In these moments, you seamlessly maintained the resonant frequency required for the attracting energy you released into the universe, setting the stage for the manifestation of your desired outcomes in the form of an opportunity. It's a powerful testament to the connection between your thoughts, the laws of the universe, and the opportunities it conspires to bring your way.

OK, now with that important information expressed, we can move on and present to you the process you can start using instantly to begin your journey of creation.

# The Process

To begin the process, we must first prime our minds to put us in the optimal state for the law of attraction. We do this by starting with what it is we want to attract. Begin by asking yourself the following question:

*"What is something I would like to manifest/attract into my life, without feeling like I need it in order to be happy?"*

**\*Note:** When you perform this, envision yourself asking this question directly to your brain. Using a mirror to perform this exercise will make it more powerful.

This question, seemingly straightforward, holds the key to unlocking your potential and desires in a unique way. Let's break down this question into its essential parts.

Part 1: *"What is something I would like to manifest/attract into my life?"*

The power of this question lies in its ability to trigger the part of your brain responsible for "instinctive elaboration." When you ask this question, your brain instinctively begins to search for an answer. This is a primal response, and it means that this question will become the primary focus of your thoughts and attention. Once you have asked this to yourself, you begin to effortlessly imagine all the things you want to attract. Because of the way these words are scripted, slipping into a state of positive visualisation is easy.

**\*Note:** *Your brain doesn't know the difference between what is real and what is imagined.*

When you vividly visualise something that you want in life, your brain reacts in a manner identical to encountering the actual manifestation of that desire. This will put you on the matching frequency of the thing you want to attract.

**\*Note:** *Imagination continued.*

The power of vivid imagination is a profound force that bridges the gap between thought and reality. In the realm of sports psychology, practitioners harness this extraordinary ability to shape outcomes by employing visualisation techniques. When we imagine an event with vivid detail, our brain responds as if the experience is occurring in real life. This phenomenon is why sports psychologists frequently guide athletes through mental rehearsals, constructing a virtual arena where success is inevitable. Through such visualisation, athletes build a repository of muscle memory for the desired outcomes, priming their minds to default to that state when faced with the actual competition (in our case, priming our minds ready for the opportunities that we attract). The brain, acting as a faithful ally, seamlessly translates the mental blueprint into physical prowess, a testament to the remarkable influence of imagination on the mind and body.

Part 2: *"...Without feeling like I need it in order to be happy?"*

The second part of the question, *"without feeling like I need it in order to be happy?"* serves an incredibly important purpose. It effortlessly detaches you from the outcome of that stated desire. This is a crucial element of this technique. By framing the question in this way, you're telling your brain that you're interested in knowing what you want to attract, without needing it to make you happy. Your brain will accept this as fact; you are confirming to yourself that your happiness is not based around this desire you have already imagined in advance. This makes it super simple to detach yourself from it and remain on the same resonant frequency as the stated/visualised desire, and this only attracts it to you even faster. This is incredibly powerful.

Part 3: *Your Desires.*

Having navigated through the foundational steps one and two, the stage is set for the manifestation journey to intensify. Once you have said the whole affirmation to yourself:

*"What is something I would like to manifest/attract into my life, without feeling like I need it in order to be happy?"*

Your mind will be effortlessly picturing all the things you want in your life (because of the way it is constructed as described above).

Now we can further cement ourselves on the same frequency as those desires. Put pen to paper and list all the goals and desires you vividly imagine in that moment, all the things you wish to bring into reality. Your mind is in the optimal state to synchronise with the resonant frequency of these desired outcomes and begin attracting them to you.

**\*Note:** While the act of listing them with pen and paper amplifies the power of this exercise and is something I recommend, flexibility is key. Whether you find yourself equipped with pen and paper or not, verbalising your goals aloud or reciting them internally is equally effective. The key here is to immerse yourself in the process with a genuine sense of positivity and joy. As you articulate your goals, let the emotions associated with each one resonate within you, embracing the satisfaction and excitement of knowing that, at this very moment, you are harmonising with the vibrational energy of the things you want to attract into your life (In the exact same way a machine resonates and attracts the same energy as its host structure when they are on matching frequencies).

Try and feel the power in this act, for it marks the convergence of intention and energy, a moment where your aspirations align with the natural frequencies of the universe. As you proceed, recognise that you are now in perfect alignment with your goals.

Part 4: *The Magic Affirmation.*

With your goals and desires written down or resonating in your thoughts, you stand at the threshold of the most important moment—the utterance of a magical affirmation that is the purpose behind ten years' work. Here it is:

*"How come I effortlessly stay on the same frequency as my goal, without needing to?"*

This affirmation, in my perspective, emerges as the keystone, the linchpin, and the most powerful declaration you can make in this process.
The profound strength of this affirmation lies in its multifaceted essence. It encapsulates the same components as step one and two, triggering instinctive elaboration and fostering detachment

from outcomes. It is intricately designed to effortlessly anchor you on the resonant frequency of any goals you have affirmed.

By posing this question to your brain, it will be focused solely on finding the answer to why you effortlessly stay on the same frequency as your goals. This complete focus is the secret to successful application of the law of attraction.

Embrace this affirmation as your new best friend, a loyal companion that consistently realigns you with the frequencies of your aspirations. Its influence extends beyond the culmination of this process. Use it throughout your day, recite it frequently, especially in moments when you sense a potential deviation from the frequency of your desires. It becomes your guide, and takes you back to the same vibrations of your goals. When you recite this affirmation, it will automatically engage your imagination to remember all the goals you have written/imagined previously, keeping you on the same frequency as them, therefore continuing to attract them to you.

This whole process is incredibly powerful because it is a unique blend of clarity, detachment, visualisation, and certainty that propels your affirmations to a higher level of effectiveness. So, constructing your words in this format operates as a nuanced yet powerful mechanism to trigger the law of attraction. Through my extensive research into the construction of impactful affirmation scripting, a fundamental understanding emerges. Initiating an affirmation with the words "What" or "How" sets the stage by posing a question to the subconscious mind, thereby activating the instinctive elaboration reflex discussed earlier. This prompts the brain into a dedicated search for answers, honing its focus on the desired outcome embedded within the affirmation. As the brain engages in solution-finding mode, effortlessly slipping into the imagination of already possessing the desire becomes second nature, imagination, a formidable force in triggering the law of attraction, takes centre stage. The final segment of the affirmation strategically detaches us from the outcome, steering away from the futile quest of when or where the manifestation will materialise. This detachment ensures that the affirmation remains on the same resonant frequency as the desire, magnetically attracting it. This process serves as a roadmap, guiding the energy in a direction conducive to manifestation.

It's crucial to note that this is not achieved through flat "I am" statements; the power lies in the careful crafting and sequencing of each element intentionally that put you on the same frequency as the desired outcome long enough to see it come to fruition.

Going back to the first part of this process for a brief moment, you may have noticed that I have provided the option of using "manifest" or "attract" when crafting the question. That is entirely a matter of personal preference; both words yield the same result. What's most important is the process of the question itself.

You can use this technique to not only manifest emotional outcomes but also for material abundance.

*Example:

Consider the following example to guide you in manifesting a material desire. Begin by contemplating what you want to effortlessly attract or manifest. Let's use a new car as an example. *"What is something I would like to manifest/attract into my life, without feeling like I need it in order to be happy?"* Pause, visualise yourself driving your brand-new car, write it out or say it to yourself in your mind, then complete the process by affirming the words, *"How come I effortlessly stay on the same frequency as my goal, without needing to?"*

You then leave it up to the universe to deliver you the opportunity for manifesting that desire. It is that simple.

**\*Important Note:**

It's crucial to remember that the transformation of mindset doesn't unfold overnight, especially if your subconscious is already sceptical. While this affirmation process is tailored to expedite the realisation of your desires, the initial days may require a measure of willpower and accountability. Consistent practice is the catalyst for change. The more you engage with this process, the more natural belief you cultivate. This belief, in turn, works to rewire your brain, rendering the process increasingly effortless over time. It's a journey of continuous reinforcement, where doing begets believing, and believing begets rewiring. As you persist in this daily ritual, you are forging a path towards a mindset and process that effortlessly attracts your desires. Once this shift becomes second nature, you'll find that the world transforms into your playground of boundless possibilities. And, when it comes to believing, always try to remember, this book is based on the real-life physics of resonating frequencies in machines that I have been working with for over a decade. Your thoughts and feelings emit a frequency, your desire resonates its own natural frequency; all we have to do is match them and keep them resonating in the same principle that we do with machines and structures.

# Ready, Set... Action

In the intricate choreography of manifestation, one key player takes centre stage: action. As explained earlier, the process outlined in this book is a symphony designed to attune you to the resonant frequency of your desires, a frequency that pulsates with the matching energy of what you want to attract into your life, and then create the opportunity for you to have that desire. Yet, understanding the subtleties of this cosmic dance is incomplete without acknowledging the pivotal role of action.

As you align your thoughts and words with the frequency of your desires, the universe responds in kind, orchestrating an intricate play of energies (in the same format I witnessed for over a decade in the machines that would attract each other's energy when resonating on the same frequency together) which will present you with a pathway to receiving your desired outcome. However, here lies a profound truth: the universe may not always deliver your desires in the exact form you envisage. Instead, as explained earlier, it often presents opportunities or gateways that resonate on the same frequency as your desire.

This is where the crucial art of taking action becomes important. Opportunities are the universe's whispers, inviting you to participate actively in the unfolding of your destiny. Acting is the bridge between the realm of intention and the realm of reality. It's the conduit through which your desires materialise, which, as already explained above, are often disguised as opportunities, experiences, or challenges that nudge you towards your ultimate goals.

The excitement lies in recognising and seizing these opportunities. Manifestation and the law of attraction are not a passive process; they are a co-creative endeavour where your actions amplify the energy you've cultivated through your thoughts and emotions.

Embrace the fun and thrill that comes with taking action, for it is in this dynamic interplay that the magic truly unfolds.

Remember, by acknowledging the importance of action, you gain the ability to spot these opportunities in your daily life. Every moment becomes a potential turning point, each day an adventure filled with excitement and possibility.

Keep in mind that taking action is not a chore; it's a choice. It can be a joyful participation in the creation of your reality. By understanding and appreciating this fundamental aspect, you not only accelerate the attraction process, but you also infuse your life with an enduring sense of wonder.

# When Do I Use This Technique

With the blueprint for constructing an affirmation that acts as a magnet for the law of attraction now in your hands, the question arises: when and where should you deploy this powerful tool? The truth is that there is no strict formula for this process. It doesn't require a designated time or place etched in stone. In my extensive experience as a practitioner of positive psychology, I've witnessed the unnecessary stress people place on the specifics of positive practices. Take journalling, for instance; individuals often fret that missing a day resets their journey towards a more positive lifestyle. Yet, when it comes to the scripted affirmation process detailed in this book, the flexibility is boundless.

Try to let go of any preconceived notions about the perfect time or place—there isn't one. Creativity is your ally here. Personally, I recite the magic affirmation—*"How come I effortlessly stay on the same frequency as my goal, without needing to?"*—in the shower, or during my morning routine, integrate it into meditation sessions, echo it on car journeys and even weave it into my gym workouts. The beauty lies in the fact that you can infuse it into any gaps in your day. Sticky notes strategically placed around your living space or phone reminders can serve as gentle nudges to keep your affirmation at the forefront of your consciousness.

If I am feeling like I want to change up my goals and manifestations then the same applies to the affirmation from parts one, two, and three of the process—*"What is something I would like to manifest/attract into my life, without feeling like I need it in order to be happy?"* If I do choose to change or add more items to my desires list, I get creative with when and where I perform this process. For me, being creative keeps it fun and enjoyable.

Now, I understand this might sound like a substantial commitment to constantly be saying this affirmation to yourself, but here's the liberating truth: there's no one-size-fits-all rule when it comes to how often you recite this either. You can choose to repeat your affirmation once a day, once a week, every hour, once a month or whenever it feels right for you. The key is to be positively creative. If you revel in the joy of reciting them every day and feel that is a routine that keeps you feeling good about maintaining the same frequency of your goal, then keep doing that. Don't forget the process is as much about enjoyment as it is about efficacy. If you do not feel good when you recite this, you are not on the right frequency. Make it fun for you.

I would consider designing a personalised ritual that resonates (no pun intended) with you, one that infuses the affirmation with a sense of joy and fun. This isn't about obligation; it's about infusing your routine with a positive energy. Get playful with it, as I described above: stick notes on your mirror, set alarms on your phone, or create a dedicated affirmation corner in your living space. The more enjoyment you derive from this practice, the more positive emotion it will generate, subsequently elevating the vibrational frequency and intensifying the attracting energy.

Trust your instincts, be creative, and make this process your own. The affirmation is not just words; it is your personal invocation to a higher level of life. So, dive in, embrace the freedom, and let the rhythm of your personal ritual guide you towards the life you desire.

# Example Templates

In the pages ahead, I have compiled some templates spanning various genres of life—money, physical health, emotional well-being, success and relationships. These templates serve as stepping stones, guiding you into the realm of intentional manifestation.

However, while these templates provide a powerful foundation when reading them, the ultimate alchemy lies in you writing them out yourself. The magic happens when you become the architect, sculpting your own words that resonate intimately with your desires and aspirations. Think of the templates as a starting point for your journey into the realms of abundance, health, success, and more.

The true potency of harnessing the law of attraction in your favour lies in your ability to infuse your personal energy into your goals. So, remember that the more you align these templates with your personal dreams, the more profound and harmonious the manifestation process becomes.

Let the below examples be your guide, your launchpad into the world of intentional creation. In the realm of manifestation, your personal goal is your ultimate ally.

Let the adventure begin!

**Money Templates:**

*"What is something I would like to manifest/attract into my life, without feeling like I need it in order to be happy?"*

Visualise the below:

- An abundant flow of money

- Financial freedom

- Prosperity

- Endless cashflow

- Unexpected additional income

Once you've finished visualising, recite the part 4 magic affirmation:

*"How come I effortlessly stay on the same frequency as my goal, without needing to?"*

## Health Templates:

*"What is something I would like to manifest/attract into my life, without feeling like I need it in order to be happy?"*

Visualise the below:

- Vibrant physical health

- Boundless energy and vitality

- Radiant emotional wellness

- Peace and presence

- Happy and healthy lifestyle

Once you've finished visualising, recite the part 4 magic affirmation:

*"How come I effortlessly stay on the same frequency as my goal, without needing to?"*

**Success Templates:**

*"What is something I would like to manifest/attract into my life, without feeling like I need it in order to be happy?"*

Visualise the below:

- Being a magnet for positive outcomes

- Triumphant achievements

- Unshakable mindset

- Continuous progress

- Powerful confidence

Once you've finished visualising, recite the part 4 magic affirmation:

*"How come I effortlessly stay on the same frequency as my goal, without needing to?"*

**Relationship Templates:**

*"What is something I would like to manifest/attract into my life, without feeling like I need it in order to be happy?"*

Visualise the below:

- Successful friendships

- A loving and caring partner

- Fun and exciting experiences with your spouse

- A happy and fun family life

- Effortless and enjoyable working relationships

Once you've finished visualising, recite the part 4 magic affirmation:

*"How come I effortlessly stay on the same frequency as my goal, without needing to?"*

OK, now that you've taken a journey through these templates, I encourage you to revisit them with a transformative twist. Engage in a mirror exercise, reminiscent of the one we explored in a prior chapter with the straightforward "I am" affirmations. As you stand before the mirror, repeat the steps in these templates, observing the profound shift in emotional connection. This whole process is designed to spark not just thoughts, but a genuine emotional resonance, evoking the feeling familiar to that of already possessing the desires outlined in each genre.

Take note of any uplifting and empowering emotions that arise; compare them to the somewhat neutral impact of flat "I am" statements you performed in the earlier chapter. This emotional shift underscores the potency of well-constructed affirmations, demonstrating how the precise wording can elevate your emotional state. If you have done this correctly you should feel the emotions of joy and excitement, optimism and belief. That is because, in the moment of reciting them, you were resonating on the same frequency as the stated goal; it was being attracted to you.

# Personal Templates

In the previous chapter we discovered that personalisation can be a beneficial key that unlocks powerful attraction. So, it's important to know that as you wield the pen to inscribe your unique desires in the tailored spaces below (covering the same genres as the previous chapter: money, physical health, emotional well-being, abundance, and success) you are not just writing; in that moment, you are scripting your future.

This chapter extends an invitation for you to become the architect of your alchemy, to infuse them with the energy and specificity that resonates intimately with your dreams. The blank spaces act as your canvas for creativity.

By completing these spaces, you're not only personalising the attraction process, but also creating a portable, personal guide that you can carry with you anytime, anywhere.

Imagine having your desires encapsulated in the pages of this book, ready to be recited whenever inspiration strikes. By filling in these blank spaces, you are not just crafting affirmations; you are curating a powerful manifestation tool that aligns with your unique journey.

**Personal Template:** *Money*

*"What is something I would like to manifest/attract into my life, without feeling like I need it in order to be happy?"*

List below, then visualise:

- 

- 

- 

-

- 

- 

- 

- 

When you've finished listing and visualising your personal aspirations, finish with the magic affirmation:

*"How come I effortlessly stay on the same frequency as my goal, without needing to?"*

**Personal Template:** *Health*

"*What is something I would like to manifest/attract into my life, without feeling like I need it in order to be happy?*"

List below, then visualise:

- 

- 

- 

-

- 

- 

- 

- 

When you've finished listing and visualising your personal aspirations, finish with the magic affirmation:

*"How come I effortlessly stay on the same frequency as my goal, without needing to?"*

**Personal Template:** *Success*

*"What is something I would like to manifest/attract into my life, without feeling like I need it in order to be happy?"*

List below, then visualise:

- 

- 

- 

-

- 


- 


- 


- 


When you've finished listing and visualising your personal aspirations, finish with the magic affirmation:

*"How come I effortlessly stay on the same frequency as my goal, without needing to?"*

**Personal Template:** *Relationships*

*"What is something I would like to manifest/attract into my life, without feeling like I need it in order to be happy?"*

List below, then visualise:

- 

- 

- 

-

- 

- 

- 

- 

When you've finished listing and visualising your personal aspirations, finish with the magic affirmation:

*"How come I effortlessly stay on the same frequency as my goal, without needing to?"*

# Signs and Synchronicities

Before we reach the concluding chapter, I'd like to go further into signs and synchronicities and emphasise the importance of approaching them correctly.

After mastering the affirmation technique and aligning with the frequency of your desire, signs and synchronicities related to that desire will start to appear in your daily life. These occurrences serve as reminders from the universe that your manifestation is in progress, reinforcing that you're resonating on the matching frequency of the thing you wish to attract.

Unfortunately, many people misinterpret these signs, leading them to deviate from the resonating frequency. For example, if your desire is a happy relationship, encountering joyous and happy couples might promote negative feelings in some, inadvertently shifting them onto the "lack" frequency.

This misunderstanding is another reason for causing scepticism about the law of attraction.

Instead, when you notice these signs and synchronicities that are on the same attracting energy as your goal, train yourself to express immense gratitude for being on the same frequency. Be incredibly happy that you've received a reminder that your goal is on its way, and patiently await the next sign. With practice, this approach turns you into a master of positive attraction, further anchoring yourself on the resonating frequency of your goals and amplifying the attracting energy.

The same principle applies to material manifestations; for example, if you're wishing to attract a new car, you may start witnessing new cars everywhere you go. Train yourself to get excited rather than feeling down about not having it yet, celebrating that you're resonating on the same frequency as your desire.

Below is an exercise designed to make signs and synchronicities enjoyable:

**Exercise:** *Signs and synchronicities tally chart*

Create a tally chart sheet covering every desire using the affirmation process in this book. Be as creative as possible to make it a positive activity. At the end of each week, reflect on the signs and synchronicities related to each desire.

Performing this exercise regularly rewires your mind to naturally look for these cues, fostering a powerful and positive mindset. It aids in overcoming the natural negativity bias discussed in the earlier chapter, making it even easier to remain on the same frequency as your desires.

# Closing Chapter

As we finish up, I want to express my deepest gratitude for accompanying me throughout the pages of this book.

My drive for the last decade has been to use my knowledge as a vibration analysis engineer and positive psychology practitioner to inspire and motivate as many people as possible to create the life of their dreams.

While we are on the topic of motivation, let's conclude and cement the essence of our exploration before we leave.

Much like the physics governing machines and structures resonating on a shared frequency, this affirmation process mirrors that resonance using the law of attraction for personal creation. Drawing from a decade of experience as a vibration analyst, I've created a roadmap in this book—a guide to aligning you with the frequency of your goals and setting in motion the attracting force that brings desires into reality.

However, the true alchemy lies in maintaining this matching frequency. Just as with machines and structures, if deviated from their resonant state, the attraction process stops. In the same principle, if we deviate our thoughts and feelings from the same frequency as our goals, we too halt the attraction process.

The outcome of maintaining vibrational resonance with your goals reveals itself as opportunities to manifest those desires. It becomes our conscious duty as creators to grasp these opportunities with action.

Belief acts as the cornerstone, fortifying the attraction. The depth of your belief directly influences the strength of the magnetic force. Commit to this resonance and watch as your goals materialise.

This is not just a theory; it's a practical guide to harnessing the law of attraction in your favour.

As you step forward, may your affirmation echo with the power to shape your reality.

*Note:

Please feel free to email me with your affirmation success story at: affirmationalchemy@hotmail.com

With heartfelt wishes,

Author, "*The Small Book About Affirmation Alchemy*"

www.ingramcontent.com/pod-product-compliance
Lightning Source LLC
Chambersburg PA
CBHW050203130526
44591CB00034B/2070